Robert's Rules of Order— Simplified

Robert's Rules <u>of</u> Order— Simplified

formerly titled
Cann's Keys to Better Meetings

Marjorie Mitchell Cann, Ph.D.

A Perigee Book

Perigee Books
are published by
The Putnam Publishing Group
200 Madison Avenue
New York, NY 10016

First Perigee Edition 1991
A revised edition of *Cann's Keys to Better Meetings*
Copyright © 1991 by Marjorie Mitchell Cann, Ph.D.

Library of Congress Cataloging-in-Publication Data

Cann, Marjorie Mitchell, date.
   [Cann's keys to better meetings]
   Robert's rules of order—simplified / Marjorie
Mitchell Cann.—1st Perigee ed.
      p.   cm.
   Reprint. Originally published: Cann's keys to better
meetings. Mobile, Ala. : HB Publications, 1990.
   ISBN 0-399-51697-2
   1. Parliamentary practice.   I. Robert, Henry M.
(Henry Martyn), 1837–1923.   Robert's rules of
order.   II. Title.
JF515.C32   1991   91-3270 CIP
060.4'2—dc20

Original cover design by Barbara Reddoch
Revised cover design by Lisa Amoroso
Text design by Tom Mason
Printed in the United States of America
1   2   3   4   5   6   7   8   9   10

This book is printed on acid-free paper.
                    ∞

PREFACE

Robert's Rules of Order—Simplified has been written in response to the frequently heard question, Where can I find a reliable book on simplified rules of parliamentary procedure?

Rather than being a compilation of the formal rules found in many published manuals, *Robert's Rules* adopts a new, simplified approach. To borrow a popular term from the computer world, *Robert's Rules* is "user friendly." It presents the fundamentals, guides you through the first steps of forming a new organization, and provides practical examples of organizational participation.

This book will help you to become more effective in your participation as a member and prepare you for leadership. You will discover that parliamentary procedure is no mystery but is simply based on common sense and common courtesy.

Officers and members of organizations have long needed a direct statement in layman's language of the correct rules of procedure. Finding none as an organizer, member and officer of voluntary organizations, I have recorded my observations of both well-conducted and poorly conducted meetings. Why are there so many differences in procedure? A careful study revealed a rather simple explanation. Too many books on this fascinating subject provide poorly written explanations and examples, as well as reports and incidents that are applicable only in exceptional cases.

In contrast, *Robert's Rules* removes all unnecessary formality and places the fundamentals of correct procedure at your fingertips.

I am grateful to officers and members of organizations in which I have been active for sharing their experiences and expertise and to friends for their encouragement. I acknowledge my indebtedness to authors of books on legal administrative procedure and especially to the late General Henry M. Robert, whose *Pocket Manual of Rules of Order for Deliberative Assemblies* was published in February, 1876. As the twenty-first century approaches, I have written *Robert's Rules* for your use in whatever society or country you may find yourself. It is my sincere hope that *Robert's Rules* will open the doors to productive and happy meetings.

CONTENTS

CHAPTER 1
Voluntary Organizations

Voluntary organizations are an integral part of the modern free world. *Robert's Rules of Order—Simplified* uses the term *voluntary* to refer to community, professional, and corporate groups and excludes parliamentary bodies of the government. Fundamentals of procedure and the decision-making process are explained to show how ideas and opinions discussed in an orderly way enable groups to reach an acceptable, majority decision.

■ A Brief History of Rules of Procedure

Since the beginning of recorded history, members of primitive tribes, communities, and nations have met in groups to deliberate and make decisions. Each group observed its self-devised rules of procedure for conducting group discussions. Frequently these rules were passed on orally to the next generation. For some years primitive tribes made records of such rules on stone, but all were formulated and preserved in ways understood by their people.

Today's accepted rules of procedure have their roots in parliamentary practices of the Roman Senate, though they have been modified through past centuries. Refinements were made when the British Parliament formulated its Rules of Procedure, but the foundations of the ancient law were not lost in the British documents. Both Canada and the United States formulated their laws and procedure primarily from the British documents. Modifications have been introduced since that time to reflect changing times and cultures.

In this country one of the first serious attempts to establish some standard set of rules of procedure for meetings at the highest levels of government was made by President Thomas Jefferson. He also recognized the need for some standards to be set for use in less formal assemblies. It was, however, many years before a manual was published with this as its major purpose. In February, 1876, Colonel Henry M. Robert's first *Pocket Manual of Rules of Order for Deliberative Assemblies* became available to the public. It has gone through many changes and editions in the past century and is recognized today as an authority on parliamentary procedure covering virtually every detail on the subject. This exhaustive exposition is appropriate for the professional parliamentarian but is not appropriate nor acceptable for the average organizational meeting. When members of voluntary organizations call for a ruling during a meeting, time does not permit one who is not an expert parliamentarian to delve into details looking for the answer.

■ Fundamental Rules of Procedure

Robert's Rules is a return to the basics of correct procedure in simplified form.

The fundamental rules require that members

1. Adopt rules of procedure for their meetings

2. Elect a chairman and a recording secretary

3. Discuss only one question at a time

4. Speak first on motions they make (with the right to speak last before the vote is taken)

5. Speak only once on a motion until all others have had the opportunity to speak once

6. Treat one another with justice and courtesy

7. Accept the rule of the majority
8. Respect the rights of the minority
9. Have equal rights

■ "Jim and Mac" on Meetings

Here's a conservation overheard at a recent meeting. "Mac" is typical of many who want to play an active part in an organization.

Jim: Hi! I notice you've been to a lot of meetings this fall. How come?

Mac: I heard we had a new president and came once to find out what was going on. Was I surprised!

Jim: Why?

Mac: They're better meetings and take up less of my evening. Lots of things are decided, too.

Jim: How's that?

Mac: Maybe you don't remember what these meetings were like last year. Let me remind you. The meetings were run by the same three or four who had run things for years, and almost no one else ever had a chance to speak. I knew the names of only two of the members, but I really can't say I knew them. Often the minutes were never read. That was typical of the lack of interest in the organization's affairs.

This year, the president has a member call the roll and has members stand and give us their names. We learn who they are, and they know who we are. What a difference! Don't you notice it?

Jim: Yes. But have you had a chance to speak?

Mac: I sure have and do you know why? The president stops anyone who has already spoken on a question and asks if anyone else wishes to speak before that person speaks again. He often calls us by name, and that is something new, too.

Jim: I noticed that. I just thought he was

3

being courteous. Has that really made much difference to you?

Mac: You bet. Don't you see how many more of us are speaking out at meetings now? I hear others' thoughts on the issues being discussed and believe I understand them better. I am enjoying meetings with the new officers running them more efficiently. You can count on my attending them regularly now.

This conversation shows why many organizations that do not observe the fundamentals of common courtesy and common sense lose members and never know the reason. "Mac" was an intelligent man who had tried to become involved in the organization and fortunately did not give up too soon. The new president came into office in time to renew interest and enthusiasm among the membership. There is little doubt that this president knew the fundamental rules of procedure and observed them.

■ Some Reasons for Joining Organizations

Vigorous voluntary organizations are essential for the exercise of free speech by free people. Active participation in voluntary organizations gives all members the opportunity to share their thoughts and express their concerns. In the resulting exchange, participants are often surprised to find that *their* concerns are the same as the concerns of *others* in the group. This offers encouragement to individuals so that action can be taken by the group, and group action is much more effective than action by an individual.

Consider an example often seen in a growing community: A factory is to be built on the vacant lot that is the only playground for children near your home. You and your family are opposed to such an idea. Now is the time for you to consider becoming a member of an action group, to express your concerns, and to share your ideas. In all probability you will discover that others in your area have the same interest in saving the playground. There may already be a local group that you can join for this purpose. If not, you may help start one to serve the needs of residents in this instance as well as other needs in the future. Apart from community concerns, a good reason for joining an organization is to develop and enhance your leadership abilities. When you identify with a group, your associates in the group hear your views and are influenced by them just as some of their views influence you. This exchange becomes a growing experience for all those involved. You will be creating a new image of yourself to others in your social, business, and professional life. At the same time, a new self-awareness will evolve, as you make new friends and grow in self-confidence. The opportunities found in small-group activities for self-expression equip a person to play more effective roles in larger groups. All this adds up to personal growth and potential leadership in your community.

In review, through membership in voluntary organizations you may

1. Discover personal and group goals that will enable you to achieve collectively what is more difficult to achieve alone

2. Gain a feeling of camaraderie and greater self-confidence

3. Increase your knowledge and skills while acquiring new attitudes for growth

4. Acquire invaluable experience for future involvement in public service

■ Before You Join

Before becoming a member of an organization you should consider its declared purposes. If you are interested in its purposes and in helping the organization work toward them, you might decide to become a member.

■ Rights and Responsibilities of a Member

When you join an organization, you have certain rights. First is the right to receive notices of the meetings, to attend them, and to participate. You may move and second motions, present resolutions, and participate as a member. You may nominate and vote for another member to hold office, as well as running for and holding an office yourself. You also have the right to take part in planning projects and undertakings of the organization. Review the constitution, bylaws, and standing rules of a particular organization to inform yourself of other rights.

As a member you also have responsibilities, such as an obligation to become familiar with the constitution, bylaws, and standing rules. You are expected to support and to help achieve the goals set for your organization. You should give your loyalty to officers and appointees, whether or not they were your personal choices. In the meetings, you must conduct yourself with courtesy toward all members. You must pay the dues required of members and other assessments determined by a majority vote. In identifying yourself as a member, you should be ready to promote the purposes of that organization at every opportunity.

■ Recommended Innovations in Procedure

Robert's Rules suggests innovations to simplify and improve the conduct of business at meetings. Some of these innovations are currently being used in many organizations; others are newer, but all are recommended in reference to procedural practices. These innovations are:

- A new division of secretarial duties
- Appointment of a publicity representative
- Precise provision for when the chairman vacates the chair and for the interval until he returns
- Simpler method for *receiving a report*
- Use of the term *to close debate* to replace the term *previous question*
- Use of the term *point of privilege* to replace the term *question of privilege*
- Use of the term *to table the motion* to replace the term *to lay on the table*
- A new category of *four special motions*

Each of these innovations is explained elsewhere in the book.

Now that you have been introduced to the fundamental rules of parliamentary procedure, it is time to move on and learn how to use them. In the following chapters, you will receive all the information necessary for formally organizing a group, preparing bylaws, and preparing a constitution, if appropriate. Election of officers and their duties, various kinds of meetings and their purposes, and committees and their reports are then discussed.

The various kinds of motions—when, how, and why each is used—are presented to show how they function as the vehicles for making decisions. The last chapter gives the final key to having successful meetings and organizations, discussing participation of members as individuals and as participants in groups. These roles differ significantly, as does your contribution in each role.

NOTES

CHAPTER 2

Forming New Organizations

When a number of individuals share a common interest and desire to consider some possible action, they should think about forming a new organization. There is perhaps no better way to learn the structure, essential procedures, and potential value of group action than to participate in creating a new organization.

■ The First Meeting

Before the first meeting someone must identify those who are interested in the same issue(s) and call them to a meeting. If this group decides to form an organization, at that first meeting they should elect a temporary chairman and secretary and designate a committee to draft bylaws and perhaps a constitution, as explained below.

Begin the first meeting by persuading someone to preside at this meeting during the election of a temporary chairman. This person moves to the front of the room and states:

> **"The meeting will come to order.
> A motion is in order for the
> election of a temporary chairman."**

This motion must be seconded and then the presiding chairman says:

> **"It is moved by Mr. Raye and
> seconded that Mr. Adams be
> elected to act as temporary chair-**

9

man. All those in favor say aye;"
(pause) **"those opposed say no."**

If the majority say no, the forming of the organization is delayed until a chairman is chosen with a majority vote. If the majority of those voting say aye, the task of forming an organization moves forward.

The temporary chairman takes the chair and states:

"The next order of business is the election of a temporary secretary."

The motion is completed as was the motion for electing the temporary chairman. The secretary moves to the front of the room and records in the minutes of the meeting the action taken by the group.

The chairman next requests that individuals in attendance state and reaffirm the purpose of the meeting. The chair should encourage discussion and then ask for a group decision in the form of a resolution, which is stated:

"Resolved that this meeting has been called to form an organization for the purpose of. . ."

A member must second the resolution; then the chair restates it and opens the meeting to discussion, debate, and possible amendment of the resolution. The assembly must adopt the resolution before attending to any other business.

The chair then asks if there is a motion to come before the meeting for a committee to draft bylaws and perhaps a constitution. The time for the committee to report back to the group should be included in this motion, and the motion must be seconded. Members of the committee may be volunteers, appointed by the chair, or elected from the floor.

When there is no further business to be discussed, the chairman may either ask for a motion of adjournment or may declare the meeting adjourned.

■ The Constitution, Bylaws and Standing Rules

The official documents of an organization historically have been a constitution and bylaws. The **constitution** contains the fundamental rules of the organization. It states the name, purpose, composition of its membership, offices, number of meetings required during the year, and approved procedure for amending the constitution. The bylaws refer to the matters of procedure. These rulings are stated as "articles" in both documents.

In recent years, many organizations have chosen to prepare only one document — the **bylaws.** This is their right, and their decision depends upon circumstances uniquely theirs. For instance, when a newly formed organization will be affiliated with a state or national one, the new organization will be required to adopt the constitution of the parent organization. The local group will need only bylaws for their official document. Another group that would need only bylaws is one that intends to be in existence for a relatively short time and that has only short-term goals and purposes.

With the thought that combining two documents into one is an easier task than the separation of one unified document into two, I present the contents for each of the separate documents in Table 1: Models of a Constitution and Bylaws.

Standing rules are of a semi-permanent nature. These rules may be established and later abolished by a majority vote and without notice. An example of the need for such a rule is when entertainment has to be planned for guest speakers: by having the rule already established, a member can be selected to assume this responsibility without further ado. Another example is a rule stating that all resolutions need to be put in writing and signed by the mover and seconder. These rules may also be amended without previous notice but with a two-thirds vote.

TABLE 1: Models of a Constitution and Bylaws

■ The constitution should contain:

Article 1.　The name of the organization.

Article 2.　The purpose.

Article 3.　Membership qualifications.

Article 4.　The offices and their election procedure.

Article 5.　Provision for an executive committee.

Article 6.　The required number of organizational meetings through each year.

Article 7.　The method of amending the constitution.

■ The bylaws should contain:

Article 1.　Membership classification, qualification, rights and duties, and termination.

Article 2.　Duties of officers and the executive committee.

Article 3.　Provisions for standing committees.

Article 4.　The frequency of regular meetings.

Article 5.　Number of members in attendance required for a quorum.

Article 6.　Provision for notification of regular and special meetings.

Article 7.　Election provisions, including time of year, methods of nominations, and installations.

Article 8.　The designation of the organization's fiscal year.

Article 9.　Standing rules and special rules.

Article 10.　Parliamentary procedure authority.

Article 11.　Method of amending the bylaws.

■ The Second Meeting

At the second meeting, the temporary officers continue to serve until the constitution and bylaws (or the bylaws only, if that was the decision of the group) have been adopted and a new slate of officers has been elected. Or if a nominating committee is formed at this meeting to propose candidates, the temporary officers continue to serve until a third meeting, when officers are elected.

The chair now asks for a reading of the minutes of the first meeting. After the minutes have been read and approved, the report of the committee on the constitution and bylaws is given. The convener of the committee orally reads the document(s) until every article and section has been heard, discussed, and agreed upon by a majority of the group. In reading this report, the convener must pause after each article so that discussion may take place.

Adoption of each document is the next order of business, although the entire report must again be read and open to discussion if the members vote to have this done. Adoption of the document is by one single motion requiring a majority vote. Only when the motion is won and the result announced by the presiding officer does the group become an official organization.

The next order of business will be election of new officers or selection of a nominating committee as presented below.

■ Procedure for the Election of Officers

The constitution should state the procedure for the election of officers. Unless this procedure is amended in the constitution, (see "Amending the Constitution and Bylaws" in this chapter) its provisions may not be suspended. The first step is to have nominations; this is followed by elections. If a nominating committee is the choice of the members, elections will not take place until there is a subsequent meeting of the association.

Nominations in voluntary organizations

should be made

1. by a nominating committee elected by a vote of the members or by the executive committee. The former procedure is preferable. Or,

2. from the floor.

■ Installation of Officers

When the initial slate of officers has been elected for the new organization, the installation ceremony takes place immediately. Since no formal procedural rules provide for this, it may be either an elaborate or a simple procedure. The outgoing president expresses appreciation to the officers and committee members for their support and accomplishments during his term of office and then introduces the installations officer. This officer next, in turn, introduces each one of the new officers, asking if they accept the responsibilities of their designated offices. The official conclusion of the installation process is when he congratulates the incoming officers and hands the gavel to the new president.

At subsequent annual meetings, the installations officer is appointed by the president or the executive committee at least a month prior to the annual meetings. Installations will generally occur on election day unless the bylaws make other provisions. As an organization increases its membership and interests, the installation process often becomes a more elaborate affair. The bylaws should provide for such changes and should make provision for other needed modifications of this nature.

■ Nominating Committees

Nominating committees are sometimes elected rather than appointed. Each system has its advocates and in small organizations, it is not at all unusual for an outgoing president to appoint the committee, but this often restricts the nomination of potential candidates. I recommend that election be the choice. This usually results in a broader selection of candidates from the entire membership. Also, an election affords less opportunity for one controlling group to perpetuate its control. Once this committee has been elected, the date of the meeting at which its report is due should be stated by the chair.

Because the future of an organization is largely dependent on the leadership qualities of its officers, there are advantages to having a nominating committee. Members of the committee will meet to discuss the nominees' potential qualifications and how those qualifications can benefit their organization. They can arrange time to consider and compare the nominees' interests and goals with those of the organization. Their conclusions should result in the best slate of candidates for each office.

■ Report of the Nominating Committee

The first responsibility of the committee is to prepare a slate of nominees. No name should be on the slate without the permission of the nominee. After the chair calls for it, the report is given, and after its reading the chair invites nominations from the floor. Nominations need not be seconded. Nominations may be closed by a member stating:

"I move nominations cease."

Or when it is apparent that there are no more nominations to be made, the chair may declare them closed by "general consent." The result of the vote on nominations is not official until announced by the chair. Voting then is held for all offices for which there are nominees. (Refer to "Procedure for the Annual Meeting" in Chapter 4.)

■ Voting

Methods:

1. **Acclamation.** Members say aye or no.
2. **Show of hands.** If there is any doubt, a count is taken.
3. **Standing vote.** A count might be needed if there is any doubt.
4. **Secret ballot.** Used mostly for elections

and important questions.

5. **Secret roll-call ballot.** All members voting place their signatures on the ballots.
6. **Roll call.** Members respond when their names are called.

When the secret ballot is used, an official count is made by the tellers or by the secretary in a smaller assembly.

Types of votes:

1. **Majority.** More than half the number of votes cast on a question.
2. **Two-thirds.** Requires two thirds of the votes cast and is used only for motions that set aside a fundamental principle of procedure.
3. **Tie vote.** Also called a casting vote because the vote is lost unless the chair casts a vote to break the tie. When the chair decides not to cast a vote, the motion is defeated.
4. **Plurality vote.** The largest number of votes cast for any candidate even though it may not be a majority. Used only when the assembly wishes to save time.
5. **Unanimous.** No dissenting vote.
6. **General consent.** The chairman assumes he has the consent of the members. It is a shortcut in voting, since it permits a meeting to take action without going through the procedure of a regular motion.
7. **Vote by the secretary.** A unanimous vote used when only one name is presented for nominations. The secretary is instructed by the chairman to cast this vote for the nominee.

■ Amending the Constitution and the Bylaws

As time goes by, members may see a need to amend articles in either the constitution or the bylaws, and it is their privilege to bring this to the attention of their organization.

A word of caution is in order here. The official documents of any organization must always be regarded as a whole, and conflict must be avoided between the provisions of both, for it is the articles in them upon which the organization is founded.

Amendments to the constitution can be made only by a two-thirds vote of the members present. Furthermore, previous written notice must be given to the members at a regular meeting at least three months prior to the meeting at which the vote is taken on the amendment.

Amendments to the bylaws are made in a similar way. The only two exceptions in the procedure are: (1) these amendments require previous notice only at the regular meeting immediately preceding the meeting at which the proposed amendment is to be considered by the members, and (2) they require only a majority vote. Desired changes may be minor or substantive; minor changes do not affect the spirit of the document, whereas substantive ones are of a major disposition and result in extensive changes. A single motion can serve to explain the minor changes proposed and should be considered and voted upon one at a time. Major changes affecting the entire document should be regarded as a revision of the document and dealt with article by article as is done when forming a new organization.

■ A Parliamentary Authority

Every organization should adopt a book on rules of procedure as its parliamentary authority. Article 10 in the models of the bylaws (Table 1) makes this provision. The adopted authority should be used to guide the organization in its deliberations on all matters not provided for in the constitution or bylaws or standing rules. This authority needs to be chosen with great care. It must be correct, and it should reflect that modifications in procedure have been continually introduced to keep the rules current with the times in which they are to be used. Although rules of procedure may be modified through the years, basic principles of parliamentary law do not change. *Robert's Rules of Order—Simplified* has been written for these contemporary times and is recommended for adoption by your organization as the authority on rules of procedure.

CHAPTER 3
Officers

■ The Executive Committee

The president, vice-president, secretary, and treasurer are the officers of an organization and form the executive committee. The immediate past-president also is a member. The president may appoint additional members, such as those who have successfully held office in past years as well as one or more of the former chairmen of standing committees. Whenever feasible, members who have worked well as officers or on committees and have shown a continuing interest and concern for the organization's success could be added to the committee.

The executive committee is an administrative committee and is elected to carry out the decisions of the majority of the members. The constitution and the bylaws should state the committee's responsibilities.

The executive committee meets at stated intervals and at the call of the chairman. It conducts interim business and prepares the agenda for meetings of the organization. Minutes of its meetings should be presented at each subsequent meeting of the whole organization. If the organization needs information on a business matter that is not readily available to the membership, the executive committee should obtain such information, then draft it, and present a summary of the information at the next regular meeting. Since the executive committee has prepared the agenda for the regular meetings as the administrative body of the organization, this committee has the responsibility to facilitate the conducting of the meeting but must never monopolize the discussions.

■ The Chairman

The chairman[1] or president of an organization presides at the business meetings and is an ex-officio member of all committees. Members address this officer as Mr. or Madam President, or Mr. or Madam Chairman. This person's conduct while occupying the chair must be impartial and impersonal. Referring to himself as "the chair" is conducive to this and is correct. Members should also refer to this person as the "chair" while he is presiding.

At meetings, the presiding officer makes certain that facts presented are clear to those in attendance, that correct procedure is observed, and that motions are completed in a reasonable time frame. Restricting the discussion to the subject under consideration enables the group to arrive at a majority decision more readily than otherwise. Yet it is important that meetings be long enough to obtain everyone's input. One recommendation is that the chair keep the discussion moving rapidly, while allowing speakers time to express their thoughts on the subject. Then prior to any vote, the chair goes around the room systematically and asks all members if they have any other points of interest for the group. In very large groups, this can be done by randomly selecting a sampling of members and asking for their views. No one person or group can control a particular discussion when an opportunity for input is offered to all who may have felt they had no previous opportunity to speak.

The chair should introduce each item of business with an impartial statement of the facts known to him. When a subject is introduced without a motion, the chair should ask if a

---

[1]For convenience, when we use the term "chairman" it should be clearly understood that it is employed in the literary sense to include both men and women. Similarly, the term "he" is used throughout the book in the generic sense to include either gender.

member wishes to make a motion before discussion proceeds. The chair should review the facts occasionally, and at the appropriate time say:

"Since these are the facts now known to us, are you ready for the question on the motion?"

The chairman should not occupy the chair if he wishes to speak for or against a motion under consideration. He must remove himself by asking the vice-president or another member to serve as chairman until the discussion and motion have been completed. At that time, the temporary chairman asks the regular chairman to resume the chair. When presiding, the chair has no vote except when there is a tie vote. The chair, then, may elect to cast the deciding vote to break the tie. The chair also may choose to refrain from breaking the tie and by this decision, the motion is defeated.

The chairman should

1. open every meeting on time or as soon thereafter as a quorum is present

2. announce in proper order the business of the meeting

3. maintain compliance with the organization's constitution and bylaws

4. request a roll call only of officers unless the constitution provides otherwise

5. have minutes presented, corrected if necessary, and approved

6. moderate discussion of all motions during the meeting, keeping the members informed on the progress

7. restate all motions clearly and ask for more clarification from the maker of the motion if needed

8. conduct a vote on all motions and announce the results

9. present acts, orders and proceedings for the organization or have them presented

3

Officers

10. sign all communications addressed to the organization

11. preside at executive committee meetings

12. act as the representative of the organization to outside persons and other organizations

■ The Vice-Chairman

The first responsibility of the vice-chairman is to be prepared to assume the chair when called upon to do so. It may be only a temporary assignment when the chairman cannot be present or wishes to take part in the discussion. Or it may be of a more permanent nature, as when the chairman resigns or dies. In either case, the vice-chairman assumes all the responsibilities, privileges, and duties of the office. In case of death, the vice-chairman moves into the office of chairman for the remainder of the term.

Bylaws and standing rules quite often designate specific areas of responsibility to the vice-chairman. These may include supervision of committees for the year or heading one critical area of work, such as being chairman of a special committee. The vice-chairman might serve as chairman of the finance committee or as chairman for visiting dignitaries. Another area of service in which a vice-chairman can make an invaluable contribution is as the publicity representative, which is described later in this chapter.

■ The Secretary

The responsibilities of the secretary are many and varied. The secretary records minutes of regular meetings, assists the chair by taking notes and being ready to elaborate or explain exactly what business is pending, conducts most of the correspondence of the organization and collects and keeps records of bills incurred prior to submitting them to the treasurer. The major duties generally assigned to one or more secretaries are:

1. Notify members of the time and place for each meeting.

2. Record proceedings of all meetings (regular and executive meetings).

3. Prepare a copy of the agenda and the order in which it is to be presented for the chairman.

4. Maintain an accurate roll call (unless this duty has been assigned to the membership chairman).

5. Have on hand the organization's constitution, bylaws and a copy of their parliamentary authority.

6. In the written minutes, give the name of the organization , the kind of meeting, date, time and place, disposition of previous minutes, business transacted, exact wording of every motion, name of the mover and seconder, results of the vote, and the time of the adjournment. The secretary must date and sign the minutes and include his title.

7. Read the minutes of the previous meeting.

8. Attend to all official correspondence.

9. Collect and record all bills before submitting them to the treasurer.

10. File all papers and documents related to the business of the organization.

11. Notify committee members of their appointments and give each convener the names of his committee members and a statement of their responsibilities.

12. Advise state and/or national head-quarters (if these are part of the organizational structure) of the names of new officers and committee chairmen upon election or appointment.

13. Hand over to a successor all records, documents, and materials pertaining to the office at the end of the term of office.

An organization with a fairly large and active membership should divide its secretarial duties. This will facilitate transaction of business and increase participation in the duties by the members. The executive committee should study the various duties required of a secretary in their organization, and, if necessary, divide the duties among two or more secretaries. A typical division of duties is:

1. **Recording secretary:** responsible for keeping all records of the meetings.

2. **Corresponding secretary:** responsible for all correspondence.

3. **Financial secretary:** responsible for receiving bills, preparing the paper work required for ongoing costs and current expenses, and submitting reports to the treasurer.

■ The Treasurer

The treasurer is the officer who receives the monies of an organization and disburses it upon orders of authorized officers. Generally the treasurer and the president are cosigners of monies to be disbursed. The treasurer should be available to facilitate financial transactions and present regular reports at the meetings. The treasurer must make an annual report and sometimes a quarterly report. The treasurer's report is not "accepted"; it is "received" at the end of each fiscal year, the treasurer's reports are audited. The executive committee should appoint a qualified independent auditor who is not a member of the organization. After the auditor presents a report at the annual meeting and the president determines that there are no questions or objections, the president states:

"A motion is in order to adopt the auditor's report."

If any serious questions arise concerning the auditor's report, the president appoints an auditing committee to investigate and report to the next meeting.

The treasurer should

1. collect monies due the organization

2. validate all vouchers presented for

payment

3. disburse money on a request cosigned by the president or other officer designated by the rulings

4. file receipts for and keep accurate records of all financial transactions

5. present regular financial summary statements

6. maintain a bank account in the organization's name

7. prepare a yearly financial report and present it to an auditor or auditing committee designated by the organization

■ The Publicity Representative

Voluntary organizations should appoint a special officer as their publicity representative to the press. One of the members — a person with experience in accurate reporting is especially good — can make a valuable contribution to the group by accepting this office. Often the business presented at meetings is of interest strictly to the membership; a non-member with no knowledge of the organization could easily misconstrue discussions and activities.

The publicity representative should discuss any prepared news release with the secretary before forwarding it to the media. In this way, only accurate and appropriate news of general interest is reported to the public.

3

Officers

NOTES

CHAPTER 4
Meetings

"We need to call a meeting," is heard more often than many of us want to hear it, yet meetings are essential and valuable. Members of associations come together to consider, discuss, and decide issues and projects. This chapter will explain different kinds of meetings and help you feel comfortable in your role as a member or a leader. Keep in mind that our simplified rules of procedure are based upon the five fundamental rules found at the beginning of Chapter 1, and you will discover that already you hold the "key" to better meetings.

■ Kinds of Meetings

Voluntary organizations will generally hold four kinds of meetings throughout the year: (1) business meeting, (2) general meeting, (3) special meeting, and (4) annual meeting. Each has its unique purpose, procedure, and agenda. The **procedure** is the sequence in which the meeting moves as it follows the agenda. Items planned for consideration constitute the **agenda** at a meeting. A secretary should send a notice of each meeting to all members in good standing.

■ Preparing the Agenda

Prior to each meeting of an organization, the executive committee plans the regular order of business and the details of the business to be considered. One of the best ways to do this is to have the committee meet for an hour or so immediately before the time of the announced

4

Meetings

meeting. At this hour, the chairman and secretary can bring before the committee a list of items on a proposed agenda for the day's meeting. Other members of the committee may contribute items they believe should be on the agenda, and the agenda is finalized.

■ Procedures for Business, General, and Special Meetings

Organizations should hold a **business meeting** at regular intervals to transact the organization's business. The procedure is:

1. The chairman says the meeting will come to order.

2. The secretary calls the roll.

3. The secretary reads the minutes of the previous meeting, which are corrected, if necessary, and approved.

4. The chairman makes announcements, which may include telegrams and correspondence requiring no action.

5. Officers report in this order: president, vice-president, secretary, and treasurer.

6. Committee chairmen report in this order: standing committees, special committees.

7. Unfinished business, including postponed motions and correspondence referring to old business from the minutes, is handled.

8. New business, such as more recent correspondence and "notices of motions" served for this meeting, is conducted.

9. The chair calls for notice of motions not previously served.

10. The meeting is adjourned.

The **general meeting** is sometimes known as the program meeting. The procedure is:

1. The chairman calls the meeting to order.

2. The secretary reads the minutes of the previous meeting, which, if necessary, are corrected and then approved.

3. Announcements are made.

4. The program is presented.

5. The meeting is adjourned.

The member responsible for arranging the program introduces it. At the conclusion of the program, an expression of thanks either formally or in the form of a motion is in order.

Special meetings may be called with short but reasonable notice to members of an organization. The notice should state the purpose of the meeting, and only the business stated in the notice may be considered at the meeting. Rules of procedure for a special meeting are the same as for a general meeting.

■ Procedure for the Annual Meeting

The annual meeting varies from the usual business meeting in that it includes annual reports and the nomination and election of officers. Written reports by the officers and chairmen must be read and then submitted to the executive committee. These written reports summarize their participation in the business of the organization during that year. Rather than the usual report of the treasurer, the report of the auditor is presented at this meeting. The usual practice is to have the president's annual address given at the conclusion of all other reports and immediately preceding the election of officers. The minutes read at an annual meeting are those of the last previous business meeting. Minutes of this current annual meeting are read at the organization's next regular meeting. The procedure is:

1. The chairman calls the meeting to order.

2. The secretary calls the roll of voting members.

3. The secretary reads the minutes; the members correct , if necessary, and approve them.

4

Meetings

4. Officers report.

5. Chairmen of standing committees report.

6. Chairmen of special committees report.

7. Auditor reports.

8. Officers are elected.
(a) When election is by secret ballot, the chair appoints two or more tellers, depending upon the size of the voting assembly.
(b) When a nominating committee has been elected or appointed, their report is now presented.
(c) The chair invites write-in nominations.
(d) The chair invites nominations from the floor. These do not need to be seconded.
(e) Officers are elected and installed.

9. Miscellaneous business is considered.

10. The meeting is adjourned.

At least a month prior to an organization's annual meeting, the executive committee or the president appoints an installations officer. This office is temporary and automatically dissolves after the installations have been completed. (Refer to" Installation of Officers" in Chapter 2.)

■ Annual Dinner Meetings

The procedure for an **annual dinner meeting** is open to variations, depending on the organization and its unique interest but the basic procedure includes:

1. national anthem

2. brief address of welcome by the president

3. dinner

4. brief introduction of prominent guests (usually those seated at the head table)

5. introduction of the speaker(s) by the program chairman

6. expression of appreciation by the program chairman

7. adjournment

■ Adjourned Meetings

A meeting may be adjourned or temporarily terminated due to adverse weather or travel conditions or other unseen circumstances, such as there being no quorum. In such a case, an adjourned meeting is scheduled. Another case for holding an adjourned meeting is when time does not permit completion of the planned agenda. The time and date for holding any adjourned meeting should be included in the motion for adjournment. The date chosen should be a date prior to the next regular meeting of the organization. When the meeting is reconvened, it continues its agenda from the point at which it was adjourned, except that minutes of the preceding meeting are first read.

Annual meetings of larger organizations have a greater amount of business on the agenda than do the meetings of smaller groups. If an annual meeting cannot be completed in one session, the postponed parts are referred to as sessions rather than adjourned meetings. One other interesting point of procedural language is that an adjourned meeting may itself be adjourned to a later time.

■ General to All Meetings

The chairman of a meeting is responsible for observing and enforcing correct rules of procedure. However, when there is an appointed parliamentarian, the chairman should request a ruling on any questionable point of procedure. The parliamentarian is there to advise and support enforcement of proper procedure whenever called upon to do so.

One reason for changing the order of business in a meeting might be when the president calls for the report of the standing committee on membership and it is not ready. If the committee chairman responds:

"Mr. President, our committee is continuing to register new members and has not had time to complete its report."

the president can ask that it be presented at the earliest possible time. Should another member raise an objection to this decision, the chair addresses the meeting by saying:

"A motion is in order to permit the meeting to proceed with the next order of business."

As with all motions, this one must be completed.

Quite often, it is possible to save time at a meeting without neglecting any fundamental rules of procedure. For example, if the executive committee deems that certain correspondence is of no interest to the membership and that it does not affect the welfare of the organization, such correspondence need not be presented at a meeting.

Whenever discussion occurs and there is no motion on the floor, the chair should remind the meeting that a motion is in order. Should a member persist in holding the floor without making a motion, the chair has the right to say:

"The member is called to order."

If discussion continues among members, then the chair states:

"The meeting is called to order."

If disorder continues, the chairman should declare the meeting adjourned and vacate the chair.

When a presiding officer permits excessive deviation from the "orders of the day" and proper and orderly conducting of business is thus prevented, any member may stand and say:

"I call for the orders of the day."

This motion requires the presiding officer to return to the agenda for the meeting.

It is permissible to suspend the orders of procedures when and only when this action does not conflict with the provisions of the constitution or the bylaws. The reason for the suspension should be stated by the chair, and instead of a formal motion to suspend the rules, the chair may ask the members for permission to conduct the business for which the suspension

4

Meetings

was requested. If, however, a formal motion is introduced for this purpose, a two-thirds vote of those in attendance is needed for it to carry.

A "point of order" may be moved by a member at any time if the member believes a violation of correct procedure has occurred. To correct the violation, the member may rise and say:

"I rise to a point of order."

The chair replies:

"State your point."

After hearing the point, the chair decides whether or not the member is correct and replies:

"Your point is well taken. Thank you." Or **"Your point is not well taken. Thank you."**

When the chair has ruled against a member on a point of order, the member may rise again and say:

"I appeal from the chair's decision."

When another member has seconded this appeal, the chair states the motion, allowing limited debate, which restricts each member present to one statement. The chair may make the first and the last statement on the ruling. If the chairman vacates the chair during the discussion to ensure impartiality, the vice-chairman presides. After this limited debate, the chairman returns to the chair and puts the question to a vote. A tie vote sustains the chair.

When a member thinks that an objectionable motion has been made, the member may address the chair and state:

"Mr. Chairman, I object to consideration of the motion."

The chair replies:

"An objection has been made to a consideration of the motion. Those in favor of considering the

33

**motion, indicate by saying 'aye';
[pause] those opposed say 'no'."**

The chair then announces the result of the vote.

Procedure was designed to make meetings productive and enjoyable. The proper use of the rules does not put obstacles in the way of free discussion by members nor does it impose itself as a direct learning experience in a regular meeting. Anyone who wishes to pursue the study of parliamentary law should arrange to meet for this special purpose. For example, a study group might plan a number of meetings. A deliberative assembly meets to transact business, not to have members display their knowledge of the rules of procedure. In all meetings, members will learn from those members who unobtrusively follow the rules.

4

Meetings

CHAPTER 5
Committees and Committee Reports

The greater part of the work of organizations is done in committees rather than during the regular meetings. This is because the average organization needs every minute of its allotted meeting time for completing the agenda of its business decisions, policy-making, and planning its future activities.

Committees have been called "the work centers of an organization." This is true, especially when a question requires research, consultation with specialists, and evaluation of the findings before a sound decision can be made.

Committees have a number of clear advantages over a meeting of the entire membership, and the greatest is their size. Being a smaller group, they have more options of places to meet, the hour to meet, and the frequency of meetings. More discussion is possible when fewer individuals are present, for each may speak frequently in exchanging ideas and information and complete the assignment more efficiently.

Rules of procedure are not as strictly enforced in committee meetings, although the fundamentals of procedure should always be observed. The chairman may take part in discussions, and members are not limited to speaking only once before all others have had the opportunity to speak. Members need not address the chair every time they speak, and they are free to ask questions during the discussion. These are some of the advantages of working in a smaller group. I believe every member should have the experience of working with others in committees before accepting an office in an organization. It is a learning experience that will help anyone become a more effective member and leader.

■ Forming Committees

Members may be elected or appointed to committees. **Election** of a member to a committee is usually reserved for large and formal organizations. Provisions for proper procedure are found in the bylaws or standing rules. The president of most voluntary groups **appoints** the chairman of the committee and requests this person to select the committee members. In some organizations the president also has the option of selecting all members of any committee except a nominating committee. When this is done, the first-named member generally serves as the chairman. It is the duty of the committee chairman to call a meeting of the committee. If, within a reasonable time the chairman fails to do so, any two or more members of the committee may call a meeting.

■ Types of Committees

Voluntary organizations have standing committees and special committees to do most of the work that can not be completed in the regular meetings. Members of standing committees generally remain in office for the same period of time as do the elected officers of the organization. Special committees are appointed for special assignments and when these have been completed, the committee is dissolved.

The bylaws of an organization authorize the standing committees and state the area of responsibility each one will serve. Some examples of standing committees are: education program, community affairs, international relations, publicity, and membership. The areas of ongoing interest and activity of your group will determine the names of your standing committees.

One of the standing committees or special committees may occasionally need to appoint a subcommittee to help with its work. For instance, in planning an annual luncheon, the committee in charge may need a smaller group to be responsible for guest invitations. The subcommittee is responsible to and reports only to that committee appointing it and is dissolved when its assignment has been completed.

■ Size of Committees

In most organizations, the actual size of a committee will depend on the nature of the assignment. Where there is a need for considerable study and research and the membership is fairly large, a committee might include as many as fifteen members. However, in a majority of organizations a committee of five to nine will usually adequately serve the organization.

■ Selection of Committee Members

There are no hard-and-fast rules on how committee members are to be chosen, but time and experience have shown that some ways are better than others. When a chairman has been selected and the selection of the committee given to him, it is recommended that he and the president together select members. By so doing, the president and chairman can share their knowledge of those members they mutually believe will make the greatest contribution.

■ Term of Office

Standing committees have assignments that arise from changes in the needs and interests of their organizations. Traditionally, these committees are terminated when the officers with whom they serve go out of office.

An alternative to this practice is herewith proposed, since many assignments are ongoing and do not neatly end when officers' terms end.

Retain two or three experienced members for a two-year term, replacing the others, so that a full complement of the standing committees exists at the beginning of each year. Then, at the end of each year, retain another two or three for a second year. This provides continuity in the affairs of the organization, which is lost when all members are terminated at the same time as the changeover of officers.

■ Assignments to Committees

The assignment to a committee generally takes one of three forms. The committee may be asked to present reports

1. only on facts relating to the assignment;

2. on the facts, together with conclusions they reach;

3. on the facts, conclusions, and their recommendations for action to the organization.

The assignments will determine the type of report it is to present to its organization when the work has been completed.

■ Reports of Committees

Committee reports should be submitted in writing, with the exception of those given at regular meetings. A report may or may not be **adopted**; it may be **filed**. The decision to adopt or not to adopt must be given consideration before any vote is taken. Once the members vote to adopt a report, they bind themselves to whatever the report recommends and to its entire content.

To file a report is an action that indicates no action will be taken at that time. It is frequently the judicious decision. By doing this, an organization receives it and makes it a part of the records, without any commitment to adopt it. At a later time when the members may want to consider taking action on the matter, the findings are available.

A routine or progress report is always filed. For example, when a committee is assigned a fact-finding study, no action is called for and the report is simply filed. Filing may also be appropriate when fact-finding and conclusions or recommendations is the assignment. The chairman of the committee or the member giving the report generally moves for the adoption of the report and its recommendation(s). However, if there are indications from the membership that postponing this decision is preferable, rules of procedure permit the mover of the motion to withdraw his motion. A motion is then in order to file the report. This allows more time to study the recommendations.

Any committee report that includes recommendations should have the recommendations at the end of the report in the form of a resolution as an integral part of the report. For further information, see chapter 6, where resolutions are discussed in greater detail.

The reports of committees may have receptions other than those discussed here, but by knowing what generally happens to a committees' report you will be better prepared if there are any unexpected or unusual developments. For instance, a report may be returned to the committee for reasons given at the meeting, or it may be rejected entirely. This is unusual, but it does happen.

■ Resignation of a Committee Member

Should it become necessary for a committee member to resign, he should address his resignation to the chairman of the committee or the president, whomever made the appointment. If the member was elected, he addresses his resignation to the committee chairman.

■ The Committee Chairman

The chairman of a committee needs a clear understanding and appreciation of the reason the organization exists. This person should become familiar with the beginnings of the organization, its goals, and the significance of these to the membership. The chairman should be well-informed of the articles of the constitution, bylaws and standing rules. Other prerequisites for the successful chairman are enthusiasm for the assignment and talent to lead and keep the group on track until it has submitted its final report.

The committee chairman notifies the president of the organization each time the committee has a report to give. Regular reports par5

on plans and progress of the committee are necessary to keep members of the entire organization well informed.

Prior to holding any meeting, the committee chairman requires some specific information relating to the assignment(s). The chairman should be given

1. a written statement of the motion referring this assignment to the committee, with specific details;

2. copies of any earlier reports on the subject;

3. any other relevant data available from the executive committee or other members.

■ A Minority Report

Suppose that some of the members of a committee do not agree with the report of the majority of the committee members. What then? Those members in disagreement should prepare what is called a minority report and notify the president. The minority report must not only be read to the assembly, but a motion must be made after the reading to have it substituted for the report of the committee. The time to make this motion is prior to any action on the committee report. If the motion to have the minority report accepted is completed and carried, it becomes the report of the committee and a motion is then in order to file the initial committee report.

CHAPTER 6
Motions

Motions fall into four general classes and one special class. Their purpose is to introduce business for consideration and possible action by members of an organization. Motions have been classified in a way that gives some of the classes a higher ranking than others. I hope to show you in the description of the motions and their applications how this facilitates the conduct of business.

■ Classes of Motions

The classes of motion are: main, subsidiary, privileged, incidental, and special. A brief description of each class of motion follows; then specific motions within each class are explained in detail in separate sections.

Main motions may be made only when no other motion is before the meeting. Only one main motion may be brought before the meeting at a time. It must be disposed of before any other motion may be considered. A motion is said to be a *pending motion* when it is before the assembly but has not yet been completed.

Subsidiary motions are applied to pending motions. These motions affect another motion that has not yet been decided by the members at a meeting. Their purposes are indicated by the names of each of the motions in the listed subsidiary motions in Table 2.

Privileged motions have the effect of requesting the chair to return to the business of the day, to recess or to adjourn, and also to set the time

Motions

41

for the next meeting. As privileged motions, they take precedence over all other motions, for each calls for some immediate decision. Privileged motions can become main motions and debatable, *but only* when no other business is on the floor.

Incidental motions consider procedural issues and are used to enforce correct rules of procedure. They arise from decisions previously determined by the group and also from the rights of members and of the group. There is no rank among these motions. They yield to privileged motions and also to the subsidiary motion "to table the motion."

Special motions are sometimes found under the class of special main motions. This is re-garded as a contradiction by some students of parliamentary procedure, and in an attempt to correct this situation, I have identified four of these as special motions. Their purpose has not been altered, and their advantages remain the same.

■ Subsidiary Motions

The names given to subsidiary motions usually indicate their use and purpose. We shall now look at the meaning and effect of these motions as used in procedure.

1. **To table the motion** is a delaying action. It permits members of an organization to post-pone consideration of a motion indefinitely. It must include a stipulation that the motion will be considered at a meeting when a majority of members are present and whenever the members desire to reconsider the question.

2. **To close debate** on a pending motion is a call for a vote on the question. This motion was known as a call for the "previous question." The term *close debate* clearly tells us that a vote in favor terminates discussion and leads to an immediate vote on the question.

3. **To limit or extend time of debate** is a motion to do just that. It is appropriate when too much time is being taken from the other business

TABLE 2.

Subsidiary Motions

(Rank 1 is highest)

RANK	MOTION	REQUIRES SECOND	DEBATE	AMEND	VOTE REQUIRED
1	To table the motion	YES	NO	NO	MAJORITY
2	To close debate	YES	NO	NO	2/3
3	To limit or extend time for debate	YES	NO	YES	2/3
4	To postpone to a definite time	YES	YES	YES	MAJORITY
5	To refer to a committee	YES	YES	YES	MAJORITY
6	To amend	YES	YES	YES	MAJORITY
7	To postpone indefinitely	YES	YES	YES	MAJORITY

on the agenda. The motion is appropriate also when the subject on the floor requires more time than is usually allotted for the discussion of one question at a meeting.

4. **To postpone to a definite time,** if passed, allows the members to consider the question either later in the same meeting or at a future meeting.

5. **To refer to a committee** assigns a question to a committee for obtaining more information before the members come to a decision. This procedure enables members to become better informed and to arrive at a sounder decision.

6. **To amend** modifies and often classifies a motion. This is to make it more acceptable to members and very often more beneficial to the organization.

7. **To postpone definitely** permits a meeting to delay its decision on a pending motion. This could be regarded as a rejection of the ideas proposed, but an affirmative vote will not necessarily prevent the question from being introduced again.

■ Privileged Motions

1. **To set the time for the next meeting** sets the time and place for the continuation of a meeting or for the next regular meeting if the bylaws or standing rules do not. It is not a simple adjournment generally, but more of a recess; hence, its classification as a privileged motion. The time set is usually a day or more later and must be prior to the time of the next regular meeting of the organization. This is in contrast to a ten-minute or an hour break typical of the usual recess in a meeting. Only after the chair announces the result of the vote may he declare the meeting adjourned until the set meeting.

2. **To adjourn** is a privileged motion in meetings of ordinary societies with bylaws providing for regularly scheduled meetings. It is generally a privileged motion for boards and committees unless otherwise stated. It is a main

TABLE 3.
Privileged
Motions

(Rank 1 is highest)

RANK	MOTION	REQUIRES SECOND	DEBATE	AMEND	VOTE REQUIRED
1	To set the time for the next meeting	YES	NO	YES	MAJORITY
2	To adjourn	YES	NO	NO	MAJORITY
3	To take a recess	YES	NO	YES	MAJORITY
4	To call for a point of privilege	NO	NO	NO	NONE
5	Call for "orders of the day"	NO	NO	NO	NO VOTE

motion and has the effect of permanently
disbanding the organization where no provision
exists for another meeting. If the motion, when
made as a main motion is defeated, it may not be
made again until after the completion of other
business.

3.   **To take a recess** is a motion that, when it
gets an affirmative majority vote, gives the
meeting a specified time to leave and a specific
time to return. When other business is pending,
it is a privileged motion. If not, it becomes a
main motion and may have subsidiary motions
applied to it.

4.   **Point of privilege** is a motion that does
not require the member making it to be recognized by the chair. The member rises and says:

**"Mr. Chairman, I rise to point
of privilege."**

The chair replies:

"State your point of privilege."

After the member states the point, the chair says:

**"Your point is well taken; the
decision is in favor of your
request** [or recommendation]**," or
"Your point is denied."**

Any two members may appeal from the decision
of the chair by using the incidental motion "to
appeal to the chair."

5.   **To call for orders of the day** is a request
to have the chair return the meeting to the
regular order of business. This motion is in order
only when no other privileged motion is on the
floor, but it may be made when another member
is speaking

■ Incidental Motions

1.   Any two members have the right to
appeal from the decision of the chair. They must
make this motion immediately after the decision
of the chair. If another motion is pending, the
appeal is not debatable; if no motion is pending

it is debatable. A tie vote sustains the decision of the chair. An appeal to the chair has certain restrictions and exceptions.

2.   **A point of order** may be called by any member when he considers that a breach of the rules of procedure has occurred. The member has the right to interrupt a speaker and need not be recognized by the chair. The chair generally states, without discussion, his determination on this point, but if he is in any doubt about the relevance of the point of order, he may refer it to the meeting. The chair says:

"The question is one of the relevance of the point of order to our ongoing discussion."

After taking a vote of the members on the relevance, the chair announces the outcome of the vote and continues with the business of the day.

3. and 4.   **Point of procedural inquiry** and the **point of information** are both questions addressed to the chair. Neither requires to be seconded, amended, or debated, nor do they need to be recognized by the chair or granted by the floor.

5.   **Suspension of the rules** is a motion that expedites the business of an organization by allowing a non-member to contribute views on a matter of vital interest to the group. Some organizations have a rule that no one but members can participate in their business meetings. However, when a guest is present who has attended a conference recently on the subject, this motion suspends the rules so the guest may be invited to present facts to assist them in their deliberations.

6.   **To withdraw or modify a motion** has one of two outcomes. If a member wishes to withdraw a motion, he is removing it from any consideration by the assembly. This may be done either before or after the motion has been seconded. Modifying a motion follows a similar process. Both procedures are discussed in this

chapter under "Getting a Motion Underway."
When the motion has been moved but not
seconded, the maker of the motion may withdraw
it by stating his decision to the chair. If the
motion has been seconded, the mover must get
the permission of the member who seconded it
before stating his decision to withdraw it. The
chair then asks:

"Are there any objections?"

When an objection occurs, a motion may be
made to withdraw or modify. This motion then
must be completed and the results announced.

7. **To postpone the reading of the minutes**
of a meeting is to deprive members of discussion
of the business conducted at a previous meeting
while it can be remembered best. It is not a
sound procedure, and if the reading is omitted,
they must be read at a subsequent meeting. An
organization may mail the minutes to members,
but even so, the responsibility of the presiding
officer is to have the minutes read at every
meeting.

8. **Consideration of a motion by paragraph**
may be requested by the presiding officer when
the motion is a lengthy one. If the chair does not
suggest that it be considered by paragraph, and it
is a lengthy motion, a member may make a
motion to have it considered by paragraph. On
the other hand, if another member thinks it
better to take the question under discussion as
one whole question in its entirety, then he should
make a motion to do so. When the motion by
paragraph has been completed and passed, the
members then discuss and amend one paragraph
at a time, if they desire to make any amendments,
until the entire document has been completed.
Then a final motion is in order for its adoption.

The basic differences between the motion "to
consider a motion by paragraph" and the motion
"to divide a question" is that in the latter, each
part of the question is an independent proposal
that can stand alone.

9. **Division of the assembly** is a call by a
member for a show of hands or for members to

**TABLE 4.
Incidental
Motions**

	MOTION	REQUIRES SECOND	DEBATE	AMEND	VOTE REQUIRED
1	Appeal to chair	YES	NO/YES	NO	MAJORITY or TIE
2	Point of order	NO	NO	NO	NO VOTE
3	Point of procedural inquiry	NO	NO	NO	NO VOTE
4	Point of information	NO	NO	NO	NO VOTE
5	Suspension of rules	NO	YES	NO	NO VOTE
6	Withdraw (Modify) a motion	NO	NO	NO	MAJORITY
7	Postpone reading of the minutes	NO	YES	NO	MAJORITY
8	Consideration by paragraph	YES	NO	YES	MAJORITY
9	Division of assembly	NO	NO	NO	NO VOTE
10	Motions relation to voting	NO/YES	YES	YES	MAJORITY

stand to confirm the count of a voice vote. This is an acceptable procedure when a member is in doubt as to whether the chair decision on the tally was correct. If the chair fails to recognize this motion, another motion is in order to take the vote by secret ballot.

10.   **Motions relating to voting** begin with nominations either by a nominating committee or from the floor. These methods are discussed under "Procedure for the Election of Officers" in Chapter 2. Larger organizations frequently elect their officers by secret ballot; this is without a doubt the best method for larger groups. The secret ballot fosters secrecy as well as independence of each member's choice. Furthermore, it prevents a nominating committee or some other small group from controlling the members' choices. On each ballot, space for members to write-in the name(s) of members other than those on the ballot is always provided.

■ Special Motions

1.   The motion **to repeal** has as its purpose the annulment of a previously adopted motion. When no previous notice of motion has been given, this motion to repeal must receive two thirds of an affirmative vote. Otherwise only a majority of the affirmative votes is required. When the vote is affirmative, it may not be reconsidered; a negative vote may be reconsidered.

2.   **To reconsider** proposes that a previously completed motion be discussed and voted upon again, but the member making this motion to reconsider must have voted with the prevailing vote. This motion can be made while another vote is pending, but no action may be taken on it until that pending business has been completed.

3.   **To take from the table** proposes reconsideration of a previously tabled motion. The effect is to permit time for further discussion and a vote on the question.

4.   The motion **to discharge a committee** has the effect of terminating the work of a committee. It will dissolve the committee if passed in

TABLE 5.
Special
Motions

MOTION	REQUIRES SECOND	DEBATE	AMEND	VOTE REQUIRED
1 To repeal	YES	YES	NO	2/3 or MAJORITY
2 To reconsider	YES	YES	NO	MAJORITY
3 To take from the table	YES	NO	NO	MAJORITY
4 To discharge a committee	YES	YES	YES	2/3 or MAJORITY

the affirmative. Since this motion would rescind action previously taken by the membership, it requires a two-thirds vote. However, there is an exception to this ruling. Only a majority vote is required for it to pass when a previous "notice of intent" has been given. If one or more members believe that the committee has failed to carry out its assignment or to carry it out in a reasonable time, this motion to discharge any or all of the members is also in order.

■ A Resolution

A more formal motion is known in procedural terms as a resolution. It is a formal opinion of a group on matters of grave concern to the membership. When the membership encounters such a problem, they will generally refer it to a committee. The committee should study the problem and then submit a written resolution stating its recommendations. It should be a definitive statement of an opinion, desire, or appeal for remedy and state clearly to whom it is addressed. It begins with "Whereas . . . ." In this preamble, there may be as many "whereas" clauses as are needed to present the reasons for the resolution, but the preamble should be as brief as possible without sacrificing clarity. The resolution concludes with the words, "Therefore, be it resolved that . . . ."

A resolution is not in order unless it is of concern to a large group of people and requires action. It is the responsibility of the executive committee to follow through and see that the recommended action is taken on all formally adopted resolutions.

■ Getting a Motion Underway

A motion is the vehicle by which a member of the organization brings business before a meeting. First, the member must "obtain the floor" and "be recognized" by the chair. To do this, the member rises or raises a hand and addresses the chair by the correct title as "Mr. President," "Madam President," "Mr. Chairman," or "Madam Chairman."

The presiding officer generally responds by stating the name of the member. At this point the member is said to "have the floor," which means that the member has been given the right to address the meeting.

The member then states the motion, saying: "I move . . . ." Some motions are seconded; others are not. If this is one that needs to be, another member does so by saying: "I second," or "I second the motion." The chairman now states the motion and opens the meeting to discussion.

If the chair does not think a motion is clear before it has been seconded, he should ask the member who has moved it to clarify it, or the chairman may modify the wording. If the chairman makes the changes, he must restate it and ask the mover of the motion whether he has now stated it so that the original intention of the motion is unchanged. Had the motion been seconded, the member who seconded it must agree to the change or withdraw his second. If this happens, another motion "to second" must be obtained before the motion goes before the meeting.

■ Completing the Motion

In discussion, the maker of the motion has the right to speak first. The maker also has the privilege of making the final remarks at the close of discussion. When it appears that discussion is over, the chair asks:

"Is there any further discussion?"

When hearing none, the chair asks:

"Are you ready for the question?"

If it is apparent that no further discussion is desired, the chair takes the vote either by voice, a standing vote, or a show of hands, and then announces the results, stating either

on favor
against
abstain

"The motion is carried" or
"The motion is defeated."

The motion has been completed when the outcome is announced by the chair.

■ Simplifying the Study of Motions

You may find yourself confused and perhaps discouraged by the study of motions. This is why you need an understanding of the fundamentals of procedure as well as an awareness that all these rules are based on common sense and common courtesy. It is advisable to take one topic at a time. Think on it until you know what it is for, its effect in meetings, and its use to members in attaining the goals they have set for themselves and their organization. *Robert's Rules of Order—Simplified* gives the basic rules for meetings. It does not require you to have all the answers to what to do or say in every instance.

This book will introduce you to procedure and perhaps even create a lasting interest in the subject. It might motivate you to go on to a comprehensive study of the subject until you become a professional parliamentarian. That is how most parliamentarians started down that road, often with no plans to do so.

Motions, their classifications, how to use them, and how they can work for you to give you better meetings have been introduced in this chapter. Just as "committees" are the work centers of organizations, "motions" are the tools for getting things done in your meetings.

The easiest way to become familiar with procedural practices is to participate. The final chapter on participation will complete your introduction to procedure and assist you in contributing more as a member and a leader.

Motions

6

NOTES

NOTES

CHAPTER 7
Participation

The dynamics of individual participation by members of organizations has been one of the most neglected topics in publications on "meetings." It has been given little if any attention by parliamentarians who emphasize expertise with formal terms and rules of procedure. This raises the question, "Without a vigorous membership actively participating in the affairs of an association, of what use is a knowledge of terms and rules?" Putting it another way, expertise without participation is like learning a foreign language but never speaking it for lack of opportunity.

Good meetings do not "just happen." Members participate in planning, contribute to carrying out the plans, and support the ongoing programs by attending meetings. Members' involvement in meetings and in the preparations for meetings make them feel they are contributing to making the organization a stronger one. As the old saying goes, "The chain is only as strong as its weakest link."

■ Why Participate?

Have you ever asked yourself, "Why do I want to participate in any organization?" There are so many possible answers to this question; some advantages that other members have found include:

1. You encounter many differences in ideas, attitudes, interests, and problems and can discuss and evaluate them.

2. You will find agreement, often after discussion, as well as mutual encouragement, inspiration, and support.

3. You will experience a new self-awareness through sharing your ideas and thoughts and a new perspective on your own thinking.

4. You acquire new insights and approaches to problems and improve your communication skills.

■ How to Participate

To explain precisely how you can learn to participate most effectively in a group requires careful analysis. A general listing follows:

1. When addressing the chair, present your ideas or information in a clear, concise, and constructive manner.

2. Remember that permission to speak a second time on a motion may be permitted only if it is to explain something in an earlier speech on the same motion *and then* only if no other member with the right to speak desires the floor at the same time.

3. Limit your speech to facts pertaining to the subject under discussion.

4. Suggest ideas and offer constructive criticism.

5. Be a good listener, so that all known facts may be presented.

6. Be willing to share in committee work.

7. If you yield the floor and are recognized by the chair, remember you have the right to resume your speech later in the same meeting.

8. Unless necessary, do not leave the room while another member is speaking; if you must leave, never pass between the chair and the speaker.

■ Group Discussion Techniques

Organizations often use group discussion techniques (1) to inform members in some depth on a subject of particular interest, (2) to stimulate an interest in and ideas on a topic, (3) to have the pros and cons on a subject presented by invited speakers.

Now that you have learned ways to participate in organizations and know the fundamental rules of procedure for meetings, it will be beneficial to become familiar with some group discussion techniques. Five techniques that have remained consistently popular are: (1) committee of the whole, (2) the six-and-six discussion, (3) the panel, (4) the symposium, and (5) the round-table discussion

■ Committee of the Whole

The committee of the whole is a committee composed of the entire membership in attendance at the time this committee is formed. It has the informality of other committees in that a freer and more spontaneous exchange of ideas and opinions occurs because rules of conducting discussion are not as strictly imposed. For instance, a member may speak to the same question as often as he can get the floor. Removing the limits on how often each member may speak tends to speed up discussion, enabling the group to consider a question in greater depth than it could otherwise.

The presiding officer of the regular meeting may vacate the chair and appoint either the vice-president or another member to take his place during the meeting of a committee of the whole. Votes taken at this committee meeting are not binding on the organization, but a report must be given to the organization after the committee has been dissolved. The secretary reads the report to the full membership, who consider it and cast their vote on any issue relating to the question. Only then is the result of this vote recorded as a decision of the organization.

Smaller organizations may choose an alternative procedure: calling for a suspension of the rule that limits each member to speaking on a question being discussed and to have the assembly move into an informal discussion. When the motion for suspension of the rules has been completed, the chair announces that the informal discussion will begin. The informality of this approach facilitates exchange of ideas and usually clarifies the issues. When the chair sees that the members are ready to return to the regular format of the meeting, he can terminate the informal discussion and call for an official vote on the question.

To create a committee of the whole, the correct motion is:

> **"I move that this assembly resolve itself into a committee of the whole."**

This motion is amendable as to length of time or a specific aspect of the general problem to be discussed. It may be debated, but it can not be referred to a committee. However, a motion is in order "to table the motion," which allows an option for later consideration.

■ The Six-and-Six Group Discussion

The six-and-six technique is used to encourage group discussion in so-called "buzz-sessions." It is a practical form of discussion and is appropriate for an assembly of any size. The name comes from the fact that groups of six individuals hold discussions on a selected topic for six minutes. It promotes discussion quickly since time is limited, and it guarantees full participation by almost every person in the groups. It gives each person a sense of belonging to the group regardless of its size.

Let us suppose that we have a convention of 600 delegates seated in a large auditorium. We wish to have a general discussion of a problem such as, "Shall this body support free university education?" We wish to have the expressed opinion of all members so that the final action will be the result of thoughtful and deliberate discussion. The chair entertains a motion that may be stated as follows:

> **"I move that we resolve this assembly into a six-and-six discussion to consider this subject of free university education for six minutes in groups of six members, one of each group being selected as recording secretary to report the group's opinions."**

This motion, if seconded, may be debated and amended. When it has been adopted, the chair says:

> **"Each row will divide into groups of three; the first three in the first and second rows will form a group of six by having those directly in front of them turn around to face those in the second row. Likewise across all the rows. For example, the third row will turn in groups of three to face the fourth row, and so on. Then, get acquainted, select a recorder, and discuss for six minutes the questions before the assembly."**

At the conclusion of discussion, the recorders shall turn in their written reports to selected ushers, or the chair may ask that the reports be prepared for reading at a later time. Reports are frequently heard from groups selected at random until a predetermined time has passed. At that time, the chair calls for them to cease and asks those in attendance if there is a motion to be made on the question. If no motion is made, the usual procedure is for the chair to request all reports be prepared and submitted to the executive committee for study.

■ The Panel

The panel is composed of a chairman and a small group of speakers—from three to seven—who have previously prepared their subject matter. The chair and members of the panel follow a question and answer format: the chairman asks questions, which different members of the panel are called upon to answer. It is customary and appropriate to have the chairman with members of the panel seated at a table on a platform before the assembly.

Since the primary purpose of a panel is to inform, the members of the panel should be specialists in the subject or specially chosen individuals who agree to study it for presentation. The panel involves group planning and group preparation, regardless of any differing viewpoints existing among the participants. After the panel has pursued the presentation for some time, the chairman invites questions from those in attendance. The questions and those of the chairman heard during the first part of the debate should fairly well exhaust all presently available knowledge of the subject. The panel's findings are now summed up by the chairman. He may then move the assembly into small groups for further discussion and when discussion ends, each group submits its findings to the chairman.

Essential to the success of a panel are well-informed participants, carefully thought-out questions, and adequate time for complete responses. The most stimulating and effective panel is one with members having distinctly different views on the subject.

■ The Symposium

The symposium is similar to a panel discussion but is more formally structured. Since it requires preparation by the individuals rather than preparations together as a group, it is sometimes preferred by the participants.

In a symposium, the chairman opens the presentation with a general introductory statement on the subject. He then introduces each of the speakers in turn who, as they are introduced, address the assembly. The number of speakers is generally five to seven, but when the subject is highly complex or controversial, there may be more speakers.

Unlike the panel, the meeting begins·with an initial speech by each member of the symposium. These are relatively brief. The meeting is then opened to a question-and-answer session among the speakers on the symposium. When discussion appears to have terminated, the chairman should summarize what has been said by the speakers. The meeting is then opened for direct exchange between members of the symposium and those in attendance at the meeting. When questions addressed to the symposium members have been answered, each speaker summarizes his own presentations and the meeting ends.

■ The Roundtable Discussion

The roundtable discussion allows issues to be presented and discussed before an assembly by individuals who are appointed either by the chairman or by a committee responsible for arranging the discussion. A leader, recorder and often a consultant may be appointed or volunteer from the three chosen to participate. The leader is responsible for planning and having the presentation prepared. Let us now consider the roles played by each of these appointees.

Success or failure of roundtable discussion is determined largely by the **leader's** ability.

The **leader:**

1. Presents the subject for discussion clearly and concisely.

2. Holds the discussion to the major issues without frustrating participation by the members.

3. Enlists the help of members to make the group "crew-minded," not "crowd-minded."

4. Summarizes and restates the major points frequently.

5. Encourages action or asks if those in attendance wish to have another meeting before any decision for action is made.

The **leader** should **not**:

1. Dominate the discussion.

2. Challenge, qualify, or comment on the ideas of others, regardless of their value.

3. Think that ability to administer parliamentary law is all that is necessary for the group process.

4. Think that a good discussion should be run with more stress on a definite plan and time schedule than on participation by all.

The **recorder** should:

1. Work closely with the leader in planning the discussion and record the plan outline.

2. From time to time summarize the points made.

3. Write a report at the end of each session.

4. Present the report, with copies for each member, at the beginning of the next session.

5. Prepare the final report with the leader's help.

The **consultant,** sometimes called the expert or the resource person, should:

1. Attend all meetings.

2. Participate upon the request of any member or of the leader.

3. Help to keep the group's attention upon the subject under discussion.

GLOSSARY

The language of procedure is uniquely applicable to the rules of procedure. This Glossary lists the terms most frequently used in meetings. They have been prepared to give you a quick reference during meetings, with concise, correct definitions and references for each.

Initially, this listing may give the impression to a new member that rules of procedure have a somewhat complex language of their own. This is only partly true. The term *motion* is one example of a word that has a different meaning in procedure and another in common usage. It is used as a procedural term to mean an "act by which a member proposes to bring a question before a group for consideration." In everyday usage, it means simply an "act" or a "movement." Then there is the term *to revoke*, which has one and the same meaning in procedure as in daily use. Practice in using the language of procedure in meetings is the best way to learn.

Accept. To give support to a report presented at a meeting. E.g., a committee report is *accepted*.

Adjourn. Terminate a meeting.

Adopt. To give approval to a motion presented to a group.

Agenda. Lists the detailed business to be considered at a scheduled meeting.

Amend. To alter a motion by a modification of the motion as it was initially worded.

Appeal from the chair. This appeal is made when any member who disagrees with a decision made by the chair wishes to have the matter put to a vote of the assembly. The member may appeal even when another member has the floor. The member rises and says: "I appeal from the chair's decision." If the motion is seconded, the chair restates the decision and allows limited debate-that is, one statement from each member desiring to speak on the motion. The chair then puts the motion to a vote. A tie vote sustains the chair.

Ballot. The secret expression of a vote. It is used for an important vote to assure confidentiality. This type of vote is frequently taken for the election of officers. When voting by ballot, the chair appoints a teller (or tellers) to pass and collect ballots and then to count votes. The chair then receives the count from the tellers and announces the name of the candidate receiving the highest number of votes. Unless the rules of the organization provide otherwise, neither the chair nor the teller(s) then, or at any other time, reveal the number of votes each or any candidate received.

Bylaws. The document that gives the detailed rulings of an organization. If it is a separate document, it ranks below the constitution but above the standing rules.

Candidate. One who is nominated or offers himself for election to an office.

Casting Vote. The vote *cast* by the chair when the vote on a motion is tied. The chair's vote is the deciding vote that breaks the tie.

Chair. The presiding officer at a meeting.

Classification of Motions. The separation of motions into classes according to their purpose and precedence.

Close Debate. This subsidiary motion stops discussion and puts the pending motion to a vote. Since it limits debate, it requires a two-thirds vote and is neither debatable nor amendable.

Committee of the Whole. The entire assembly of members in attendance at a meeting (see Chapter 7).

Constitution. The written document stating the fundamental laws and principles of an organization.

Division of the Assembly. A request that may be made when the count of a vote is not certain and a recount is necessary. The member calling for the division need not be recognized nor rise; he simply states: "I call for a division of the assembly."

Executive Committee. A committee composed of the elected officers of an organization and the immediate past president. In large organizations, two or more specially selected members are sometimes also appointed.

Executive Secretary. The secretary of an organization, usually under contract and salaried. Responsibilities are found in the bylaws when an organization employs this officer.

Ex-officio Officer. One who holds an office as ex officio because of having previously held office in the same organization. E.g., a former president might be an ex-officio officer of an executive board.

General Consent (Unanimous Consent). A shortcut in voting, which should not be used for controversial decisions. It permits a chairman to take action on a proposal on the assumption that it has the approval of the members. Examples are methods of voting and also adjournments. If there are any objections, a formal vote is taken.

Has the Floor. This means that a member has been recognized by the chair, and it is the member's privilege to speak at that time.

Honorary Members. A person who is invited to become a member due to outstanding achievements or fame. Generally this is not recommended for voluntary organizations but is reserved for professional associations. However, there is no rule prohibiting this custom.

In Order. What is being initiated or done is correct from a procedural point of view.

Majority Vote. More than half of the votes cast.

Meeting. An assembly of persons meeting for a time during which they do not separate, or they do not separate longer than for a recess of a few minutes. In contrast, a series of meetings, such as a convention, are called *sessions*.

Motion. A proposal made to the members of an organization for their consideration and action.

Obtaining the Floor. The term used to describe the situation in which a member rises, addresses the chair, and is recognized.

Objection to Consideration of a Motion. A motion to prevent discussion on a main motion. If an objection is made, it must be done before any discussion has taken place on the motion. This requires no seconder and may be made when another member has the floor.

On the Floor. This term indicates that a motion "on the floor" is being considered by a meeting.

Order of Business. The ordered sequence of business for a meeting.

Pending Motion. A motion on the floor that has not yet been completed.

Personal Privilege. A request by a member to have an item of some concern to himself as a member of the organization considered by those in attendance at the meeting.

Point of Information. A request that is made when a member desires clarification of details. The member may interrupt a speaker and need not obtain the floor.

Point of Order. A motion that a member makes when an error occurs in correct procedure. A member rises and says: "I rise to a point of order." The chair then says: "State your point of order." If the chair accepts the point as valid, the chair says: "Your point is well taken." If the chair rejects the point, the chair says: "Your point is not well taken."

Point of Privilege. A privileged motion concerned with the welfare of the total meeting, such as the physical comfort of those in attendance, or the reputation and integrity of members, either present or absent.

Proxy or Absentee Voting. Transfers a member's right to vote to another person. This is not recommended for the average voluntary organization; it is designed for representative assemblies and stock companies of shareholders.

Putting the Motion. To call for a vote on a motion.

Question. When called for, indicates that a member is ready to vote on the question being considered in the form of a motion. It does not necessarily close discussion but often expedites the voting.

Quorum. The number of members who must be present in order to transact legally the business of any organization. A majority of the members is required unless otherwise stated in the bylaws.

Receiving a Report. Having a report read to a meeting. It does not mean that the meeting approves the report or takes any official action on it.

Reconsider a Motion. May be called for when a motion has been passed and additional members enter the meeting or more information is available for presentation. Its effect is to recall the adopted motion to the floor for further discussion and another vote of the members.

Repeal. A motion to revoke a former action by the group. It may completely remove the motion that originated the action. It may or may not include that the former motion be "struck from the records."

Resolution. A formal written proposal for action by a group. It is introduced by the word *resolved.*

Rules of Order. Rulings that an organization may see fit to add to from time to time in order to govern its proceedings. They guide meetings in following the approved correct procedure.

Session. One of the meetings occurring as part of a convention.

Special Committee (ad hoc). A committee appointed to carry out a special assignment. When its assignment has been completed, it submits its report and the group is instantly dissolved.

Special Meeting. A meeting called for a special purpose. Notices are sent to all members with the purpose for the meeting stated in the notice. Only that purpose stated in the notice may be considered at this meeting.

Special Orders. A class of "orders of the day." They take precedence for consideration over all motions except another (previously made) special order, or a motion for adjournment or questions of privilege.

Standing Rules. Rules made by the governing body of an organization to control its administration. One example is setting the time and place of meeting. These rules are for serving unique needs of the organization.

Suspension of Rules. Requires a general consent vote. It is useful when it is to the advantage of the meeting. E.g., if an objection is made by a member, he may make a formal motion to change the order of business, and a two-thirds vote is required to sustain the objection.

To Table a Motion. Serves to delay the consideration of a motion. Although this motion is intended to return the motion being tabled before the members later, it can be used as a delaying tactic to prevent or discourage any further action on the matter.

To Take from the Table. To remove from the table a motion that has been previously tabled. It may be made at the same or a later meeting. This returns the motion for further consideration; it is neither debatable nor amendable, it can have no subsidiary motion applied, and it takes precedence over any main motion.

Teller. One who collects, counts, and records the number of ballots cast.

Two-thirds Vote. This means two thirds of all votes cast. It is used for all motions that restrict full and free discussion. Such motions may (1) suspend the rules, (2) repeal, (3) close nominations, and (4) close debate.

Voluntary Organizations. Those associations formally organized as community, corporate, and professional organizations, excluding all governmental bodies. Membership is voluntary.

ABOUT THE AUTHOR

Marjorie Mitchell Cann, Ph.D., is an outstanding educator and international author. Her academic studies include mathematics and English at Acadia University in Nova Scotia, statistics and administration at Michigan State University, and the Ph.D. program in teacher education at Harvard and the University of Michigan.

Dr. Cann has held positions as teacher and administrator in public and private schools, and universities in Canada and the United States. In retirement she continues to be a world traveler, play some golf, and pursue her writing career.

Robert's Rules of Order—Simplified is the result of many years as a member, officer, and organizer of organizations. Dr. Cann has become a respected consultant in this field as well as giving leadership seminars for corporate, educational and other community associations. She knows from experience that a knowledge of the basic rules of procedure makes better meetings. All unnecessary formality has been removed as the fundamentals of correct procedure are placed at your fingertips. One reviewer says that "Cann is a priestess of logic and this handbook is a treasure."